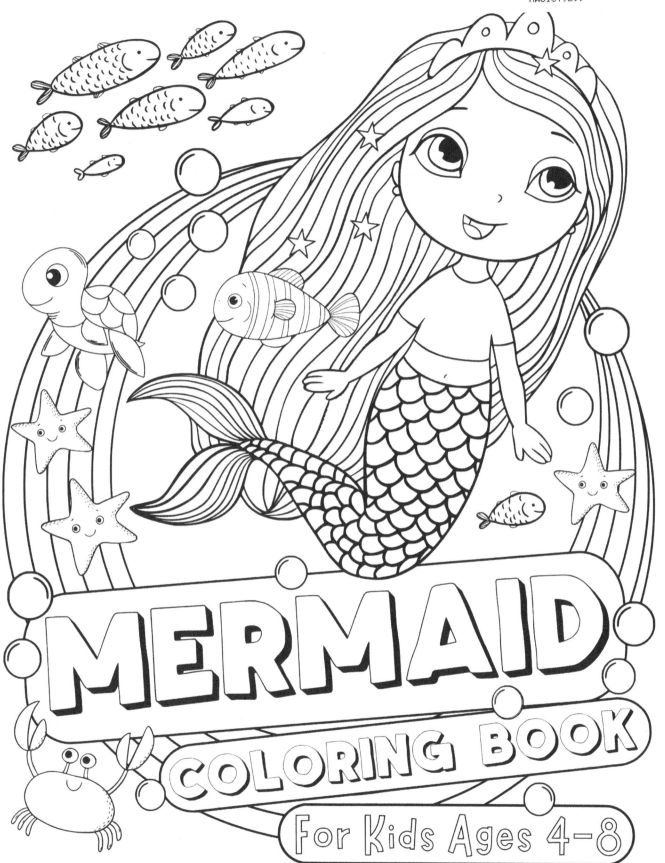

# MERMAID
## COLORING BOOK
### For Kids Ages 4-8

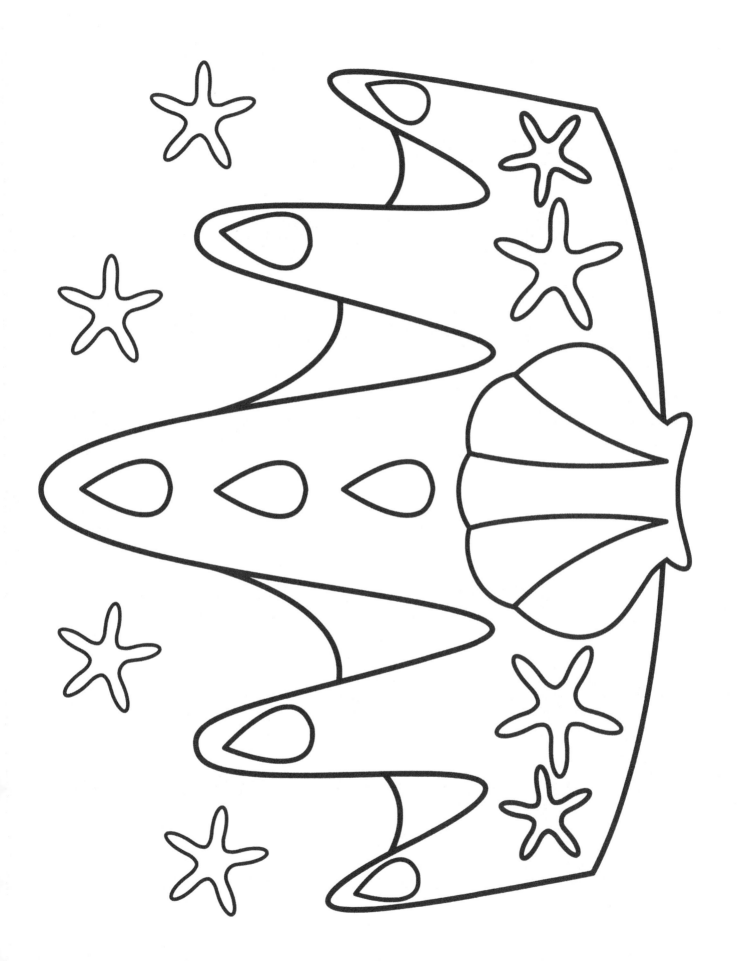

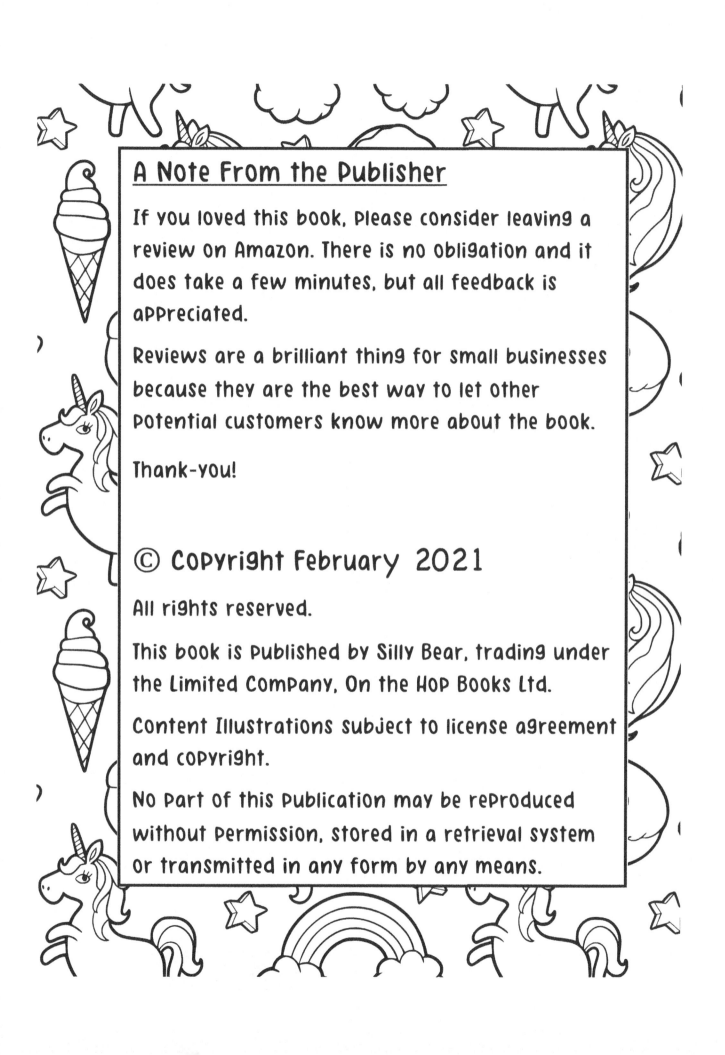

## A Note From the Publisher

If you loved this book, please consider leaving a review on Amazon. There is no obligation and it does take a few minutes, but all feedback is appreciated.

Reviews are a brilliant thing for small businesses because they are the best way to let other potential customers know more about the book.

Thank-you!

Made in United States
North Haven, CT
25 November 2021

11520899R00057